The Entrepreneurial Mindset: Strategies for Success

How to Think and Act Like a Successful Entrepreneur.

John W. Venture

I0490537

Dedication:

To my family and friends, who have supported me every step of the way.

Table of Contents:

Introduction

Introduction

Entrepreneurship is an inherently risky endeavor. Starting a business requires a leap of faith, a willingness to take on uncertainty, and the ability to navigate setbacks and failures. Despite these challenges, entrepreneurship remains a dream for many people, a path to independence, creativity, and financial success.

But what separates successful entrepreneurs from those who fail? What traits and characteristics do successful entrepreneurs share, and how can they be cultivated and developed?

The answer lies in the entrepreneurial mindset. The entrepreneurial mindset is a way of thinking, a set of beliefs and attitudes that guide entrepreneurs through the challenges and uncertainties of starting and growing a business. It is the foundation upon which successful businesses are built.

This book is a guide to developing the entrepreneurial mindset. We will explore the core traits and characteristics shared by successful entrepreneurs, such as resilience, adaptability, and risk-taking. We will also examine common challenges and obstacles that entrepreneurs face, such as self-doubt, burnout, and decision-making under uncertainty, and provide practical strategies and exercises for overcoming these challenges and developing a growth mindset.

Through real-world case studies and interviews with successful entrepreneurs, we will analyze the strategies and techniques used by these entrepreneurs to achieve success in their businesses. We will also explore the importance of innovation and failure in entrepreneurship, and provide strategies for building a culture of innovation and using failure as a learning opportunity.

Whether you're a seasoned entrepreneur looking to take your business to the next level or an aspiring entrepreneur just starting out, this book will provide you with the tools and insights you need to unlock your potential for success. So let's dive in and explore the entrepreneurial mindset together.

II. The Foundation of the Entrepreneurial Mindset

Entrepreneurship requires a unique set of skills and qualities that set successful entrepreneurs apart from others. These traits and characteristics form the foundation of the entrepreneurial mindset. By cultivating these qualities, you can develop the mindset that will guide you through the challenges and uncertainties of entrepreneurship.

Resilience

Entrepreneurship is a journey filled with ups and downs, setbacks and failures. Successful entrepreneurs possess a strong sense of resilience, the ability to bounce back from setbacks and keep moving forward. To develop resilience, it is important to reframe failure as a learning opportunity and to practice self-care to avoid burnout.

Adaptability

The business landscape is constantly evolving, and successful entrepreneurs are able to adapt to changing circumstances. This requires a willingness to experiment, take risks, and pivot when necessary. To develop adaptability, it is important to embrace experimentation and be open to new ideas and perspectives.

Risk-taking

Entrepreneurship is inherently risky, and successful entrepreneurs are willing to take calculated risks in pursuit of their goals. This requires a willingness to step outside your comfort zone and to be comfortable with uncertainty. To develop a risk-taking mindset, it is important to practice making decisions under uncertainty and to build a support network of mentors and advisors who can provide guidance and feedback.

Passion

Passion is the driving force behind many successful businesses. Successful entrepreneurs are passionate about their work and are able to maintain their enthusiasm and focus through the ups and downs of the entrepreneurial journey. To cultivate passion, it is important to align your business goals with your personal values and to stay connected to your purpose and mission.

Persistence

Entrepreneurship requires persistence and the ability to keep working toward your goals, even in the face of obstacles and setbacks. Successful entrepreneurs are able to maintain their focus and energy over the long term, even when progress is slow. To develop persistence, it is important to set clear goals and to break them down into manageable steps, celebrate small victories along the way, and stay connected to your vision for your business.

By cultivating these foundational qualities, you can develop the entrepreneurial mindset that will guide you through the challenges and uncertainties of entrepreneurship. In the next chapter, we'll explore common challenges and obstacles that entrepreneurs face and provide practical strategies for overcoming them.

III. Overcoming Common Challenges and Obstacles

Entrepreneurship is a challenging journey filled with obstacles and setbacks. To succeed as an entrepreneur, it is important to be prepared for the challenges that lie ahead and to have strategies in place for overcoming them. In this chapter, we'll explore some common challenges and obstacles that entrepreneurs face and provide practical strategies for overcoming them.

Self-doubt

Self-doubt is a common challenge that many entrepreneurs face. When starting a business, it's easy to question your abilities and whether you have what it takes to succeed. To overcome self-doubt, it's important to focus on your strengths and to remind yourself of your past successes. It can also be helpful to surround yourself with a support network of mentors and peers who can provide encouragement and feedback.

Burnout

Entrepreneurship can be a demanding and stressful journey, and burnout is a real risk for many entrepreneurs. To avoid burnout, it's important to practice self-care, such as getting enough sleep, exercise, and time off. It's also important to prioritize your workload and delegate tasks when possible.

Decision-making under uncertainty
Entrepreneurship is full of uncertainty, and making decisions can be challenging when you don't have all the information you need. To improve your decision-making skills, it's important to embrace

experimentation and to view failure as a learning opportunity. It can also be helpful to seek out feedback and advice from mentors and peers.

Building a team

As your business grows, you'll need to build a team of employees and collaborators. This can be challenging, especially if you're used to working alone. To build a strong team, it's important to prioritize communication, collaboration, and trust. It can also be helpful to create a clear vision and mission for your business that everyone can align around.

Scaling your business

Scaling your business can be a challenging and complex process. To successfully scale your business, it's important to have a clear growth strategy in place and to be prepared for the operational and logistical challenges that come with growth. It's also important to continue to prioritize customer satisfaction and to maintain the core values and mission of your business.

By being aware of these common challenges and obstacles and having strategies in place for overcoming them, you can build resilience and develop the entrepreneurial mindset necessary for success in entrepreneurship. In the next chapter, we'll explore the importance of innovation and failure in entrepreneurship and provide strategies for building a culture of innovation in your business.

IV. Building a Culture of Innovation

Innovation is the lifeblood of entrepreneurship. To succeed as an entrepreneur, it's essential to continually develop new ideas and products that meet the needs of your customers and stay ahead of your competitors. However, fostering a culture of innovation can be challenging. In this chapter, we'll explore why innovation is important and provide strategies for building a culture of innovation in your business.

Why innovation is important

Innovation is critical for the long-term success of any business. It enables you to stay competitive, respond to changing market conditions, and meet the evolving needs of your customers. By continually innovating, you can create a sustainable competitive advantage and drive growth for your business.

Creating a culture of innovation

To foster a culture of innovation in your business, it's important to create an environment that encourages creativity and risk-taking. Here are some strategies for building a culture of innovation:

Encourage experimentation: Encourage your employees to try new things and experiment with new ideas. Provide them with the resources and support they need to pursue their ideas.

Embrace failure: Failure is an inevitable part of innovation. Encourage your employees to view failure as a learning opportunity and to share their failures with the rest of the team.

Prioritize collaboration: Innovation often requires collaboration between people with different skills and perspectives. Create opportunities for your employees to collaborate and share ideas.

Celebrate success: When an innovation is successful, celebrate it! Recognize the contributions of the team members involved and share the success with the rest of the organization.

Encouraging innovation from your employees
Innovation doesn't just come from the top. It's important to encourage innovation from all levels of your organization. Here are some strategies for encouraging innovation from your employees:

Provide training and resources: Provide your employees with the training and resources they need to innovate. This could include workshops, access to innovation tools, or mentorship programs.

Create an open-door policy: Encourage your employees to share their ideas and feedback with you. Be receptive to their ideas and provide them with constructive feedback.

Reward innovation: Recognize and reward employees who come up with innovative ideas. This could be through bonuses, promotions, or other incentives.
By creating a culture of innovation in your business and encouraging innovation from all levels of your organization, you can foster a mindset of creativity and problem-solving that will drive your business forward.

In the next chapter, we'll explore the importance of networking and mentorship in entrepreneurship and provide strategies for building a strong support network that can help you succeed as an entrepreneur.

V. The Role of Failure in Entrepreneurship

Entrepreneurship is a challenging and often unpredictable journey. Even the most successful entrepreneurs face setbacks and failures along the way. However, it's important to recognize that failure is not the opposite of success, but rather an essential part of the entrepreneurial journey. In this chapter, we'll explore the role of failure in entrepreneurship and provide strategies for embracing and learning from failure.

The importance of failure

Failure is a natural part of entrepreneurship. It's through our failures that we learn and grow, and ultimately become better entrepreneurs. Failure teaches us resilience, grit, and the ability to bounce back from setbacks. It also provides valuable feedback on what works and what doesn't, which can help us refine our strategies and approach.

Embracing failure

To embrace failure, it's important to shift your mindset and view failure as a necessary and valuable part of the entrepreneurial journey. Here are some strategies for embracing failure:

Reframe failure: Instead of seeing failure as a negative experience, reframe it as a learning opportunity. Ask yourself what you can learn from the experience and how you can use that knowledge to improve your approach.

Take risks: To succeed as an entrepreneur, you must be willing to take risks. Accept that some of your ideas will fail, and use those failures as opportunities to learn and grow.

Seek feedback: Seek feedback from customers, mentors, and peers to gain valuable insights into what's working and what's not. Use this feedback to refine your approach and improve your products or services.

Learning from failure

To truly learn from failure, it's important to approach it with a growth mindset. Here are some strategies for learning from failure:

Analyze your failures: Take the time to analyze your failures and identify what went wrong. Use this information to refine your approach and improve your chances of success in the future.

Experiment and iterate: Use your failures as opportunities to experiment and iterate on your ideas. Try new approaches and test them with your customers to see what works.

Celebrate progress: Celebrate the progress you've made, even if it's not the success you were hoping for. Recognize the hard work and effort you've put in and use it as motivation to continue pushing forward.

By embracing failure and learning from it, you can develop the resilience and grit needed to succeed as an entrepreneur. In the next chapter, we'll explore the importance of building a strong team and provide strategies for hiring and managing employees.

VI. Case Studies and Interviews

One of the best ways to learn about entrepreneurship is by studying the successes and failures of other entrepreneurs. In this chapter, we'll explore the importance of case studies and interviews in understanding the entrepreneurial mindset and provide some examples of successful entrepreneurs to learn from.

Importance of Case Studies and Interviews

Case studies and interviews are an excellent way to gain insight into the entrepreneurial mindset. They provide real-world examples of the challenges and obstacles that entrepreneurs face, as well as the strategies and approaches they use to overcome them. By studying these examples, you can gain valuable insights and inspiration for your own entrepreneurial journey.

Case Studies
Here are a few examples of successful entrepreneurs and their stories:

Sara Blakely, founder of Spanx: Sara Blakely is a self-made billionaire and the founder of Spanx, a women's shapewear company. Blakely's story is one of resilience and determination. She started Spanx with just $5,000 in savings and faced numerous rejections before finally getting her product into stores. Today, Spanx is a global brand with millions of loyal customers.

Elon Musk, founder of SpaceX and Tesla: Elon Musk is a visionary entrepreneur who has founded several successful companies, including SpaceX and Tesla. Musk's story is one of relentless ambition and a willingness to take risks. He has faced numerous setbacks and failures along the way but has persevered through his unwavering belief in his vision.

Jeff Bezos, founder of Amazon: Jeff Bezos is the founder and CEO of Amazon, the world's largest online retailer. Bezos's story is one of innovation and customer obsession. He started Amazon as an online bookstore and has since grown it into a global powerhouse, with over 200 million Prime members worldwide.

Interviews

In addition to case studies, interviews with successful entrepreneurs can provide valuable insights into the entrepreneurial mindset. Here are a few questions to consider asking during an interview:

What inspired you to become an entrepreneur?
What were some of the biggest challenges you faced along the way?
How did you overcome those challenges?
What are some of the key qualities that you believe are important for entrepreneurs to have?
What advice do you have for aspiring entrepreneurs?
By studying the stories of successful entrepreneurs and conducting interviews with them, you can gain a deeper understanding of the entrepreneurial mindset and learn valuable lessons for your own entrepreneurial journey. In the next chapter, we'll explore the importance of building a strong network and provide strategies for networking and building relationships.

In conclusion, entrepreneurship is a challenging but rewarding journey that requires a unique mindset and approach. It involves taking risks, being innovative, and persevering through failures and setbacks. However, by cultivating the entrepreneurial mindset, overcoming common challenges and obstacles, building a culture of innovation, and learning from the experiences of successful entrepreneurs through case studies and interviews, you can increase your chances of success as an entrepreneur.

Remember that entrepreneurship is not just about starting a business, but it's also about creating value, making a positive impact, and pursuing your passion. It takes a combination of hard work, dedication, and a willingness to take risks and adapt to change. With the right mindset and strategies, you can achieve your entrepreneurial goals and make a difference in the world.

So, whether you're an aspiring entrepreneur or an established one, remember to continue learning, growing, and taking calculated risks to reach your full potential. And always remember, the entrepreneurial journey is not just about the destination but also about the experiences, lessons, and growth along the way.